When the Earth Was Bare

When the Earth Was Bare

Retold by Judith Witters and Kathleen Cammarata
Illustrated by Kathleen Cammarata

On a night of the Young Seal Moon, an old grandmother gathered the children close.

Long ago, the Earth Mother held us all in Her lap. We hunted and played and slept. But the earth was bare, and our People grew hot and tired. There were no trees and there were no flowers. There was no shade. And there was no beauty. Our People grew sad.

"Wise One," the People begged their chief, "go to the Maker. Give thanks, but say that we are sad."

Wise One travelled to the Maker. "Maker," said Wise One, "our People are sad. And they are hot."

"Ah," smiled the Maker, "see what I will give you."

The Maker strode wide over the plains and through the mountains, with the wind in each step.

Trees grew in the footprints. Great forests danced and whispered. Tangled flowers rustled and laughed. Cool grasses murmured. The People played and hunted in the windy forests of the Maker's footprints, and they were happy.

Summer passed. In the Moon of the Hunter, frost came. The heads of the flowers drooped. The fingers of the grasses stiffened. The leaves of the trees turned bright with colour.

With the Moon of New Ice, the leaves fell. They sang soft songs as they dropped to Earth Mother. The People cried.

"Wise One," the People begged their chief, "go to the Maker. Give thanks for the beauty of the trees and the flowers. But say we are afraid. The trees grow bare. The earth is still. What have we done to make this happen?"

Wise One went to the Maker and said, "Our People are afraid. Beauty is dying. What have we done to make this happen?"

The Maker smiled, "You have done nothing to make this happen. This is the way of things, but see what I will give you."

The Maker began to blow softly. Winter winds rustled the dead leaves. Each leaf became a bird. Golden willow leaves changed into bright finches. Curly oak leaves became round robins. Brilliant tanagers and cardinals flew up from red maples. Sparrows, chickadees, and wrens crept out of small, brown leaves.

The People clapped their hands as birds filled the air and settled on the bare branches of the trees.

The Maker said, "These are birds. They are yours. Sing with them. Learn their ways. Care for them."

The People understood. They gathered around the bare trees and thanked the Maker.

Spring came. In the Moon of Running Sap, ice melted. The Maker breathed warm winds. The grass grew green again, and the trees unfolded tender leaves.

The People learned the ways of the birds and cared for them. They sang their many songs. And the People were happy.

That was long ago.

The old grandmother stopped speaking. She hugged the children close, and whistled a different tune for each child.

And soon their songs filled the night air of the Young Seal Moon.